Balloons

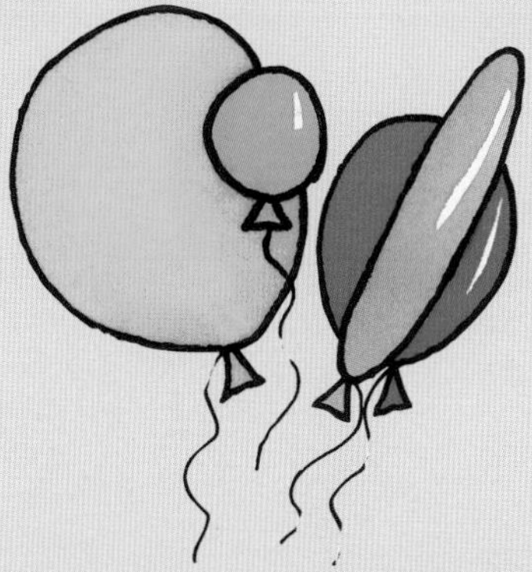

Alison Hawes

Illustrated by Woody

Rigby®

A Harcourt Achieve Imprint

www.Rigby.com

1-800-531-5015

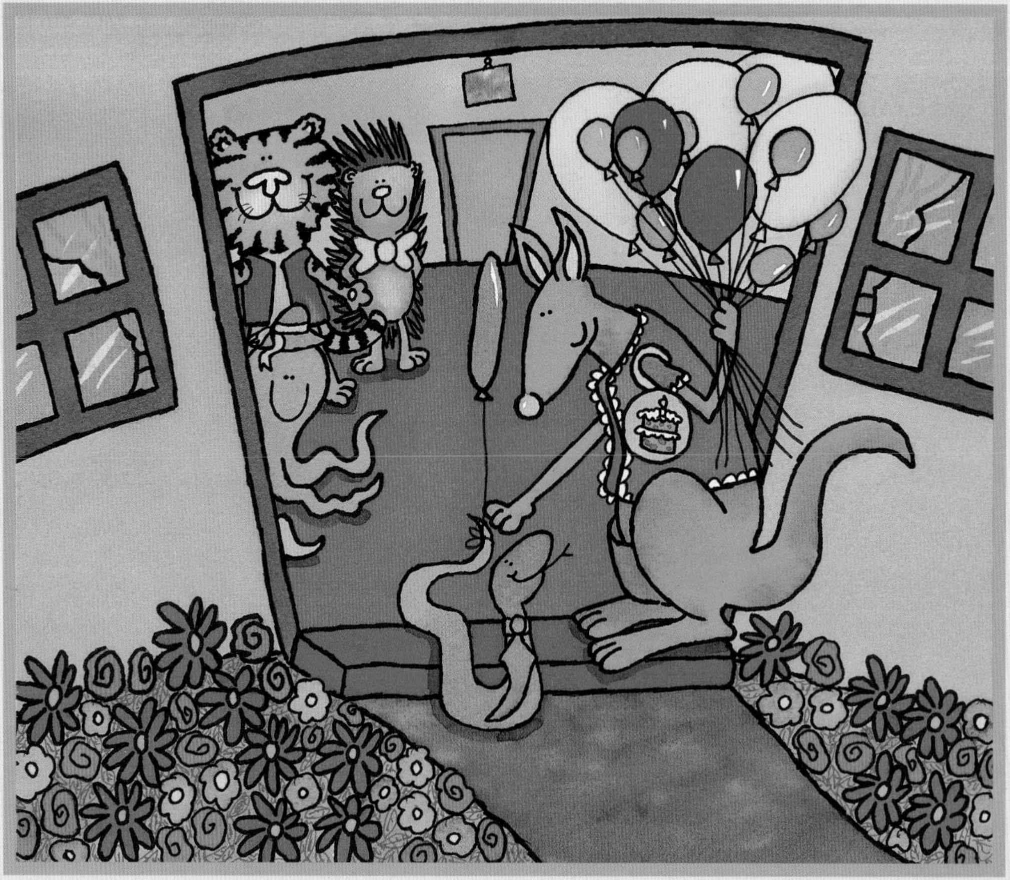

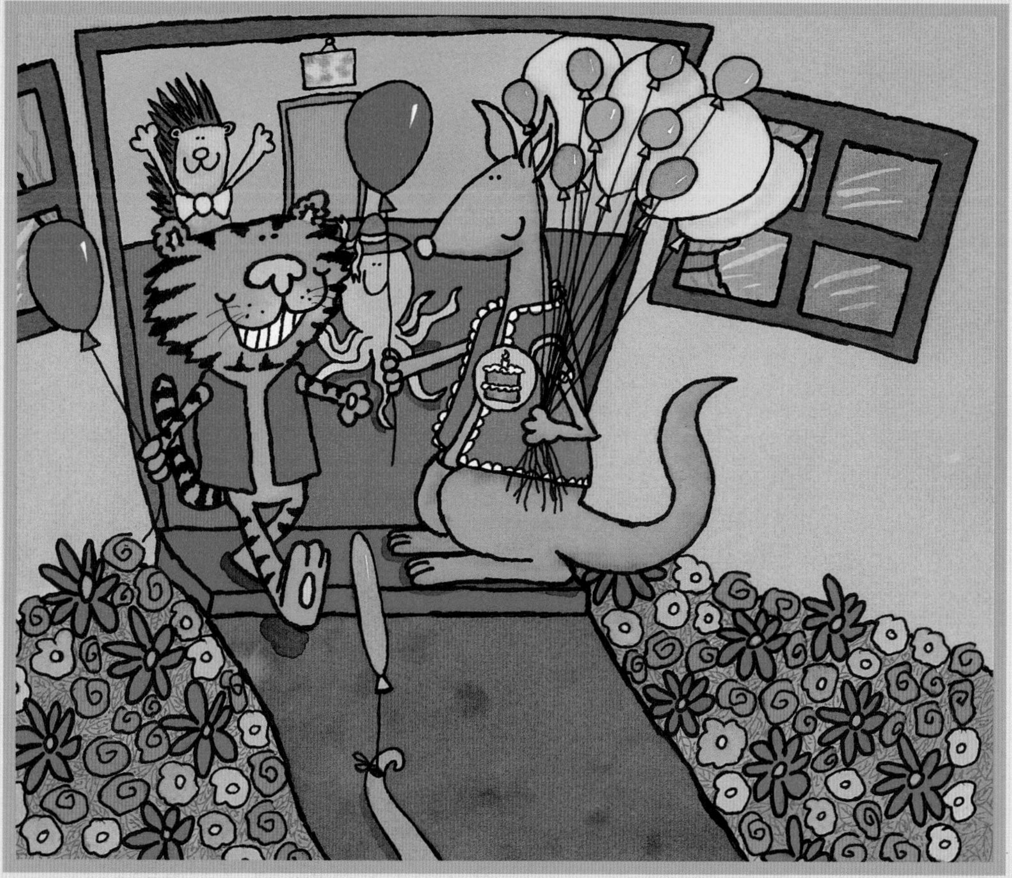

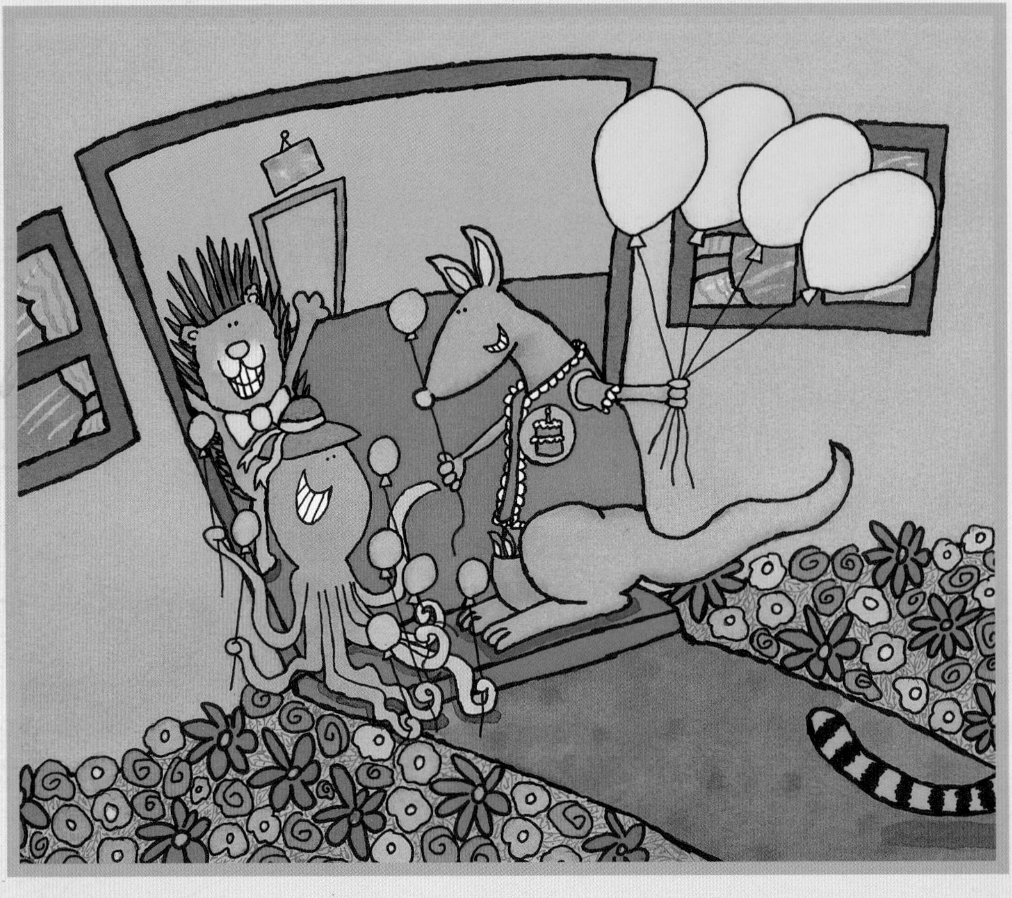

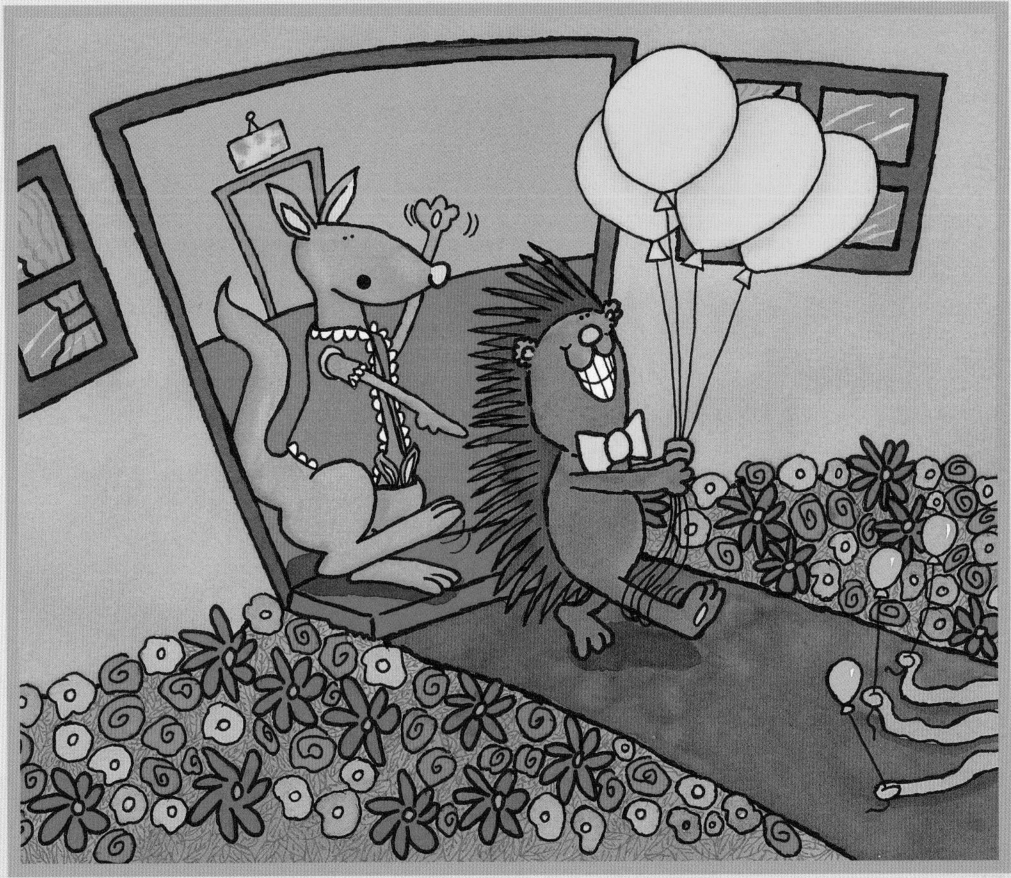

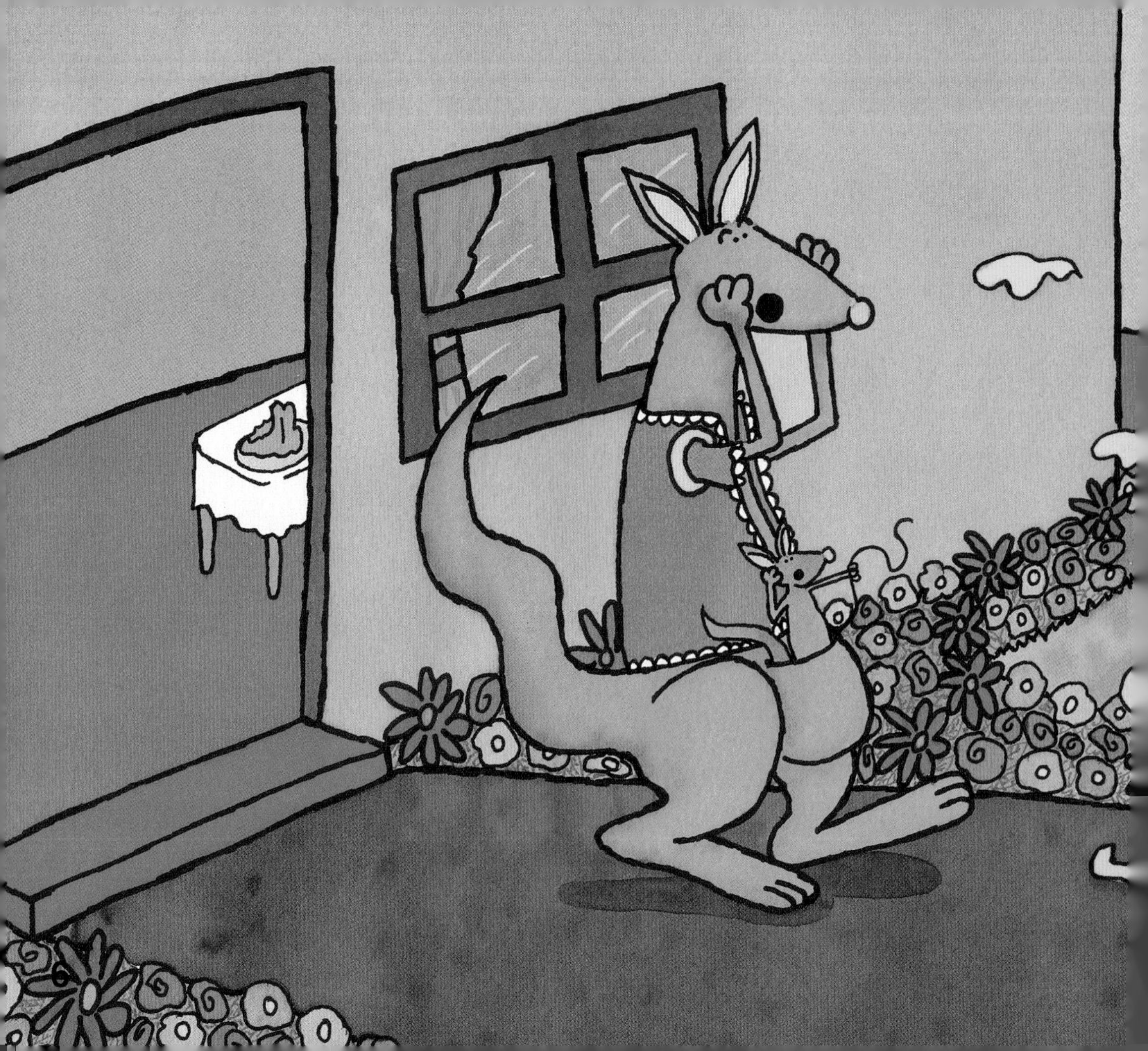

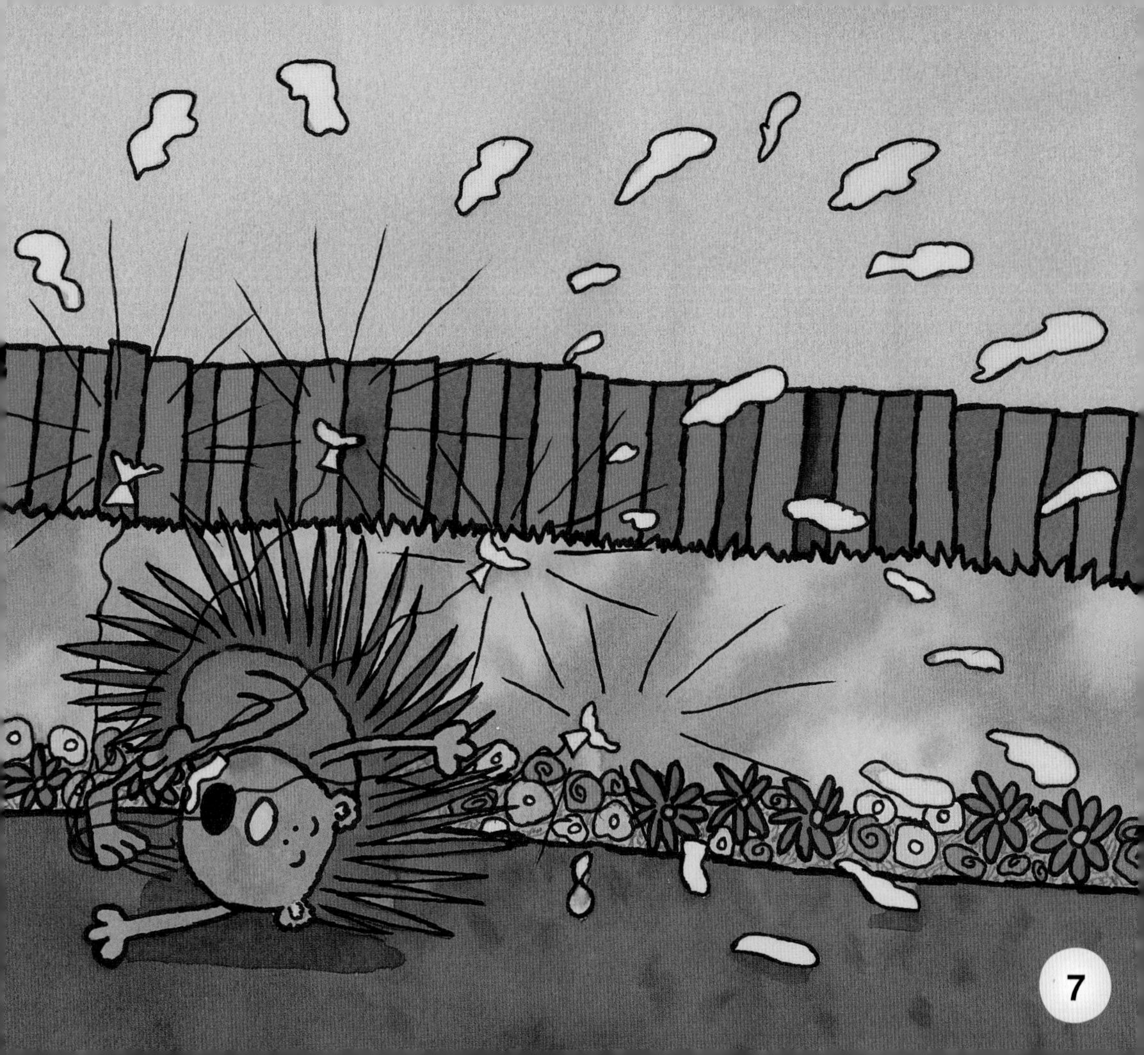

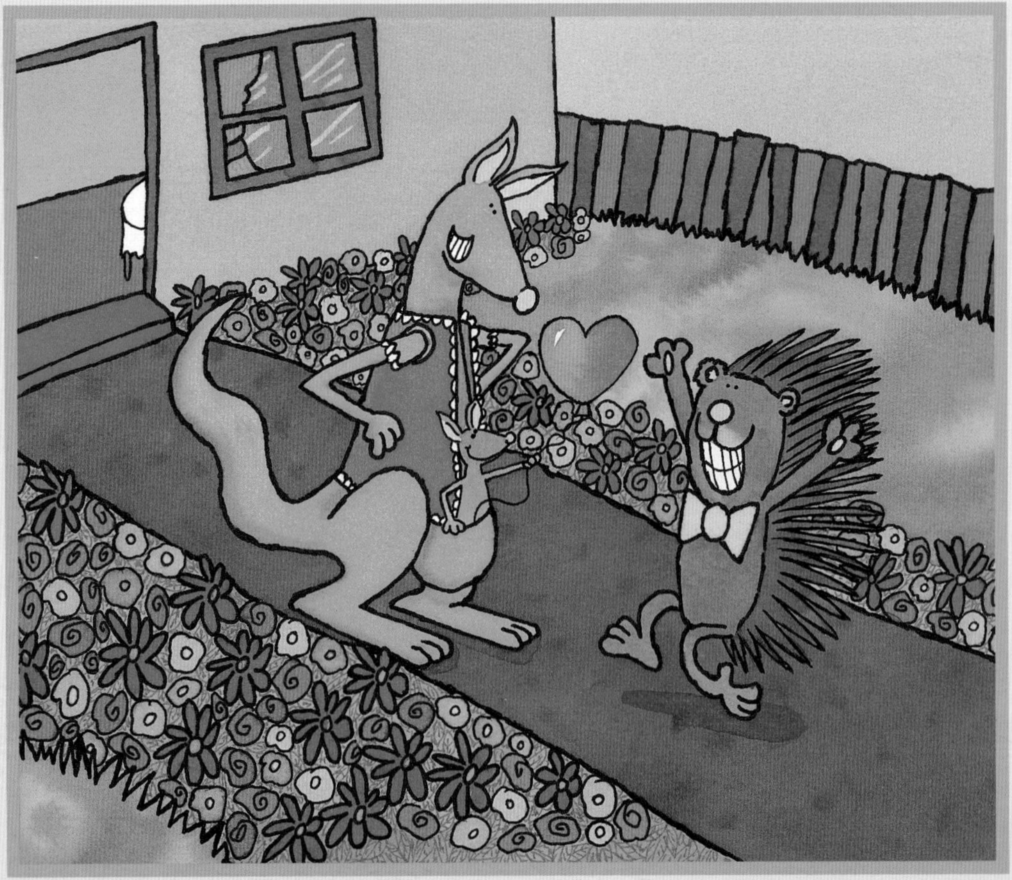